It's Not About Me

By

LLT

authorHOUSE®

AuthorHouse™
1663 Liberty Drive
Bloomington, IN 47403
www.authorhouse.com
Phone: 1 (800) 839-8640

Published by AuthorHouse 04/14/2016

ISBN: 978-1-5049-7420-2 (sc)
ISBN: 978-1-5049-7419-6 (e)

Print information available on the last page.

Any people depicted in stock imagery provided by Thinkstock are models,
and such images are being used for illustrative purposes only.
Certain stock imagery © *Thinkstock.*

This book is printed on acid-free paper.

Foreword

Sometimes you find yourself talking in circles or contradicting your thoughts. That is because you are searching for answers that you have not yet translated into questions. You feel alone, stranded in a world you cannot make sense of. I know how that feels, because I've felt like that at a very young age and pondered why was I here and was there a purpose for my life. I also wondered who are these people surrounding me, I know, I call them mother, father, sister and brother but my ways were not their ways and vice versa.

I remember one sunny morning when I was just a toddler riding my tricycle on the porch, it was a large porch with steps in the middle. I wanted to get off that porch so I decided to ride the tricycle down the steps headed somewhere, anywhere or just nowhere. I soon discovered I had made a bad decision that would be the beginning of many to come.

I was inspired to write this book because I had uncovered a flaw in my life. I was a *Racist* and a *Bigot*. I have always felt that everyone has some grain of prejudices within themselves but I did not know how deeply mine was rooted. Once God had uncovered my flaw, I cried like a baby, especially when I informed my family and friends. When I did, I could feel that nagging pain, scorning heat, anger, hatred and rage seeping out of me. Hatred for everything bad that had happen in my life, my parent's life, my sibling's life and my ethnic heritage. It was a discovery that God brought to my attention at a prime age of 59, and then afterwards, God gave me a clean heart.

James 5:16 Confess your faults one to another, and pray one for another, that ye may be healed. The effectual fervent prayer of a righteous man availeth much. (kjv) (affirmation)

Growing up on the eastside of Detroit in the 60's was an exciting time. The neighborhood was racially mixed where I lived, caucasians and blacks got along fine. Although, toward the latter part of the 60's the neighborhood became predominately black and there was no meeting of the minds between the two ethnic groups. However, at this point, in time in my neighborhood, everything was okay. I even had a caucasian boyfriend, if that is what you would call it, at a young age. Together, we were determined to change the world as it relates to racial indifferences. One day my beau and I were walking, on the side of his house, he lived several houses from mine. We were trying to decide what to do, when suddenly he leaned over and kissed me. It was just a peck on the lips, but I thought it was so romantic. He smiled and I smiled then I heard one of my siblings calling me. I told him I would see him later and ran home. I thought no one saw us but his brother did and told his mother. After that romantic encounter I saw less of him. I would knock on his door to see if he could come out and play but his mother would tell me no and then suddenly they moved away. I assume he would write me because we were in love, but he never did. As in all things, life goes on and with that so did the neighborhood.

The neighborhood ethnicity became predominately black. Many businesses, grocery stores and caucasian families were moving out. Malcolm X murdered in 1965 and shortly thereafter, in 1968, Martin Luther King (MLK) assassinated. The death of two Black leaders brought about a controversy within me, particularly in the difference between being murdered or assassinated. The news reporter made it seem a travesty the assassination of MLK as opposed to the murdering of Malcolm X. To me it was one in the same, they both died from the hands of a killer. Due to their death, Black America has resorted to looting and rioting in Detroit. The State enforced Martial Law. A curfew were setup for residents to be off the streets by 10:00 pm. Also, the National Guard were patrolling the predominate black areas where the rioting and looting originated. I was overwhelmed by my ethnic group anger, which precipitated in pillaging our neighborhood and it heighten to the burning down of stores, houses and businesses. Were my brother's and sister's conscious of whose neighborhood they were destroying? *(Which was our)* If so, where did they think our people would shop for food, clothing and services? *(If not in our neighborhood, where when we had no transportation)* Once upon a time, the neighborhood looked attractive then turned poorly now it was just a mess. There were burned down buildings and gaps where businesses, stores, or houses use to be. I do not think their action was well thought out, for it was derived from, an irrational group of angry individuals in a violent emotional state of mind. As far as I could decipher, Black folks were making it difficult for themselves. It was okay to mourn the deaths of two Black leaders in a positive productive method. Retreat with current leaders and develop a way to express their frustration in a nonviolent matter. Well no one was asking me my opinion.

As the smoke in the neighborhood simmered, I heard folks talking about two drugs cocaine and heroin infiltrating our area, causing people to do crazy things. Most of the people in the neighborhood began to resemble skeletons or zombies digging through garbage for pop cans to cash in for drugs, sleeping in condemned or vacant houses, and some drug dealers using them for shelter or manufacturing drugs or drug usage. There was this evil spirit circling our neighborhood and it seemed as if it could not be stopped. That is when I knew my goal was to get out, leave Detroit, before it overtook me.

One day, a group of men was going through our neighborhood, they were talking about a man called Jehovah. These men said you could get whatever you wanted from Jehovah all you had to do was believe in him. I said what? Get whatever you want? Where is he and why can't I talk to him? If that was all I had to do was believe well I can do that! I started asking questions and suddenly the family started going to church.

My family was large, a total of nine, and I was the middle child, to make things worst we were stair steps. My oldest brother dropped out of High School, my next older brother graduated and it seem like all our relatives were present at his graduation. I had previously attended summer school two years ago so I was a half of a semester behind him. I loved school so I went to Summer School for the fun of it. Therefore, my brother graduated in June, and then I graduated that upcoming January. You could just imagine what type of reception I received. None of my relatives were present. Of course, I was upset but I decided that maybe my relatives could not attend my graduation service? As I reflect, that seems to be a reoccurring incident for many events, in my life. However, nothing compared to the introduction of the man called Jehovah (God) and his son Jesus. It was an exciting experience and still is to this day. Not only did God give you what you wanted he gave you what you needed, and all I had to do was **ASK**. Every Sunday my siblings and I went to Sunday school at the largest Baptist church in our neighborhood. When we can home my parents would have supper waiting for us, sometimes we would bring a friend home. Mama cooked so much food we could have had the neighbor come and eat. The kids in the neighborhood, called our home the house of plenty. It felt good to give to others that did not have, but I knew we did not have much it just appeared that way. What I learned about Jehovah my God in the scripture:

Matt 7:7 *"Ask, and it shall be given you; seek, and ye shall find; knock, and it shall be opened unto you:" kjv (belief)*

So began my journey to ask for what I wanted from God in his son Jesus name. I started buying blessing candles and lighting them nightly for God to bless my family. I began to dream and saw visions of myself living in a large house with all my brothers and sisters happily and joyfully. No, our family did not have much but that which we had was enough. No, I did not ask for riches or treasures just small things such as a pair of shoes, a breast endowment but before that a training bra. Everything I asked for from God he granted it and I felt special. As I entered my teens, my parents allowed us to attend Church sermon services on Sunday. Therefore, after Sunday school, we had a break before Church sermon and we would go to the store across the street and get candy. During the sermon, my friends and I would eat our candy in the back of the church. I learned later that the Sunday school class my brothers were in the teacher would make them empty their pockets and take all their money. This left a sour note in their hearts for Church and God so they opted out on attending Church sermons. If I had known that was happening to them I would have said something to somebody, it just was not fair.

I got heavily involved in everything at the Church. I was known as a writer and started writing short skits of faith and when the Pastor got wind of it, he put my talent to use. He would have me write a skit and perform it before his sermon one Sunday out of the month how awesome was that. Life could not get any better and yet the neighborhood was continuously changing. When new families moved in the neighborhood I would greet them and befriend their children and invite them to my Church. One day after service a group of us kids was walking home and we heard tambourines, drums, guitars coming from the corner building, down the street from my church. We had never heard it before so we decided to investigate this noise. When we entered the building, we saw people dancing around the pulpit, bodies of individuals laying on the floor with a sheet over them. Then suddenly a woman was in my face saying praise the lord. Apparently, I had walked down to the pulpit where the dancing was going on while everyone else was still at the door. I remember hearing someone say grab her and I was dragged out, but I never forgot that experience. I felt like this church had God's spiritual power and this was where I belonged however the direction to achieve that goal was not clear. God started dealing with me through dreams. In my dreams God let me know I would raise my sister's children, I saw myself with 4 boys; one day my oldest brother and youngest sister would live with me; at the age of 30 I would buy a Cape Cod home, it would have brown carpet and hard wood floors; and that money would be falling out of trees all around me. I never told anyone about this because I did not think any one would believe me, but I believed. Later in life, I compared my life dreams to the story of Joseph in the bible he was one of the 12 tribes of Israel. Joseph, son of Jacob, mother Rachel, brother Benjamin was a tattletale and a dreamer. **Gen: 37:1-36** As children you sometimes do things that are not good and you don't want your parents to know so you make a bond between those involved so that everyone is on the same page and it becomes a secret. Even if our parents found out, we would continue to lie. Well I was a dreamer and a tattletale, not on all things, but on situations I thought my parents should know so it would not come back to bite them. In **Gen: 37** Joseph told his brothers about his dreams, one in particular that they would bow before him. This did not sit well with his brothers and they got angry and began to hate him especially since he was their father's favorite, and now they were going to bow down before him they wanted to kill him. One day Jacob sent Joseph out to where his brothers were to gather information and when Joseph got there his brothers ambushed him and sought to kill him, but Reuben, intervene for Joseph. He convinced his brothers to place Joseph in a pit, so later he could remove him and bring him home. However, later that day while Reuben was not present a band of Midianites merchantmen passed by and Judah one of his brothers took the opportunity to persuade the others to sell Joseph to the Ishmaelite. When Reuben returned to the pit, Joseph was not there.

Rom 8:28 "And we know that all things work together for good to them that love God, to them who are the called according to his purpose." kjv (God's will)

Joseph told his brothers years after the incident when he was ruler in Egypt also a provider for his family that he was not angry with them for what they had done.

Gen 50:20 "But as for you, ye thought evil against me: but God meant it unto good, to bring to pass, as it is this day, to save much people alive." KJV (faithfulness in Gods word)

Sometimes it is not wise to inform others what God has revealed unto **YOU**. It may cause a conflict between you and others by them looking at you with jealousy and indifference.

Entering Junior high school was scary because the building was so large and had long corridors. I felt, as I could get lost and never find my way out. I questioned why we had to go to a different school especially away from home. I could walk to our Elementary school but now I had to catch a bus with strangers! That was when I discovered that I feared change not that I couldn't adapt but that change brought about fear within me something that I had to overcome in life, and trust in the Lord God almighty.

I John 4:18 *"There is no fear in love; but perfect love casteth out fear: because fear hath torment. He that feareth is not made perfect in love." kjv (trust)*

Attending school was one of the highlights of my life I loved going to school. Even when I was sick, because I had so much fun but unfortunately I was a sickly child. I would wake up in the morning feeling great and then strange things would occur. For instance, I would start throwing up after I ate breakfast and then everything I ate. I went to the clinic and the doctor prescribed a liquid medication, I had to take twice a day and the symptom went away. I remember in the 4th grade I stayed out of school most of the semester with an illness. The doctor informed my mother I had to refrain from anything that would cause me to become hyper. Shouting, running, jumping and climbing trees, all the normal things I did because I was a tomboy, was forbidden. No outdoor activities, so I began to read every book, magazines I could get my hands on. The doctor prescribed a green syrup, I had to take, after 2-3 months I was permitted to return to school. One morning I woke up and discovered small bumps/hives was all over my body, normally they would appear at night and disappear before morning, this time they did not. I felt great but looked terrible so I did not go to school that day and the next day they were still present so I was sent to the clinic. The doctor diagnosed me as having too much acidity in my system. The doctor gave me a list of food items that had acid in them and told me it was okay to eat but I must watch my acid intake. What was funny to me the doctor asked if I liked chocolate, I said yes, he then said I would have to reduce my chocolate consumption. What he did not know was I had been sitting in the reception area eating chocolate raisins.

I had gotten over my fear of changing schools and now I was in High school. I participated in just about everything High School had to offer. I was the Senior Class Treasurer; Homecoming Queen Court - 3rd runner up; Tennis Team - wasn't that good dropped out; Field Hockey and Drama Club. I had decided I would become an actor at a young age because I was a natural. I had one boy friend while in high school and we started dating while I was in the 11th grade. We almost met two years prior it was as I was walking home, after getting off the bus. I looked across the street and there was this young man walking. He looked built and he walked with a purpose. I was over come by his presence then he suddenly entered the house slightly directly across the street from my house. I had never seen him before and I wondered if he was a visitor because I knew the people who lived in that house. I did not meet him until 2 yrs later, I gave him a Valentine card with kisses and wrote on the back of the kisses you can cash them in and he did. At that time, I mentioned to him the first time I saw him, he said he remembered but he did not like the street we lived on. He would stay at his cousin's house during the week and came home on the weekends. He also said he asked his brother about me. I knew then he was the ONE for me. We became high school sweet hearts, had a long distance relationship for over 20 years, then he got married, divorced and married again, and produced three children. I never quite got over him, he was the love of my life and I would size every man up to his standards. No one could meet his standards when I compared them to him. You know, it takes time to nurture a meaningful relationship one that has trust, commitment, understanding and love, naturally as well as spiritually.

I Psalms 1-6

Psalms I: 1-3 "Blessed is the man that walketh not in the counsel of the ungodly, nor standeth in the way of the sinners, nor sitteth in the seat of the scornful. But his delight is in the law of the Lord; and in his law doth he meditate day and night. And he shall be like a tree planted by the rivers of water, that bringeth forth his fruit in his season; his leaf also shall not wither; and whatsoever he doeth shall prosper." kjv (living spiritually granted natural blessings)

Up until the age of 18, I was a natural born liar. I never was caught lying became it was normal for me. My parents wouldn't allow us to go and hang out so, I would tell my friends a lie about not being able to go to football, basketball, baseball games, night parties or going over to some of their homes. I knew it was wrong but I never was caught I guess my remembrance in what I said to an individual worked well. When I graduated from High School I decided to stop lying, it just was not necessary and College would be a fresh start. I also realized that I was not living in the present world but a world I had created and it was centered on me for my well-being. I felt like a little princess because everything worked out for me all the time. God was good to me and I praised him all the time.

The steps to enroll into College was nerve wrecking because I didn't have a great grade point average but I applied to five Universities and was accepted to them all. One of the five applications was to the College my boyfriend was attending. However prior to discovering my acceptances, my High School Counselor informed me that my best option would be to accept an offer to attend a summer program at a certain University north of Detroit, which would prepare me for College life. If I did accept, the program I would automatically be accepted at the University in the fall. I told my Counselor I had to think about this, but then my boyfriend informed me that he had received his draft card and had to drop out of College, to enlist in the Army. He served two years and when he returned he applied to become a police officer, which was his life long dream. Now, it was my time to accept my counselor's option or wait to see if I received acceptance from the other Universities. I based my decision on my boyfriend draft notice; I accepted the offer north of Detroit. All through this process not once did I ask God for direction. Maybe, I thought God would not help me I really do not know what I was thinking. Therefore, off to the University I went unsure of myself because now I was on my own in a sense. There would be no one to help me get up each morning; tell me when to go to bed; who to hang out with; what to say or watch my tone when speaking to an adult. Would I remain the sweet God-fearing girl that I was raised to be? I guess only time would tell.

Arriving at the University, you check-in, and are issued a room with a roommate. My roommate was from Detroit she was cool and all but within the first week, she had met a boy and fell in love, now they were shacking in our room. Even through the dorm was coed alternate floors this was upsetting to me and uncomfortable. I wanted to report this to someone anyone but I did not. The entire winter semester I lived with an additional roommate. I finally suggested to my roommate that she should discuss rooming with her boyfriend's roommate girlfriend and then they could have a room to themselves. The next semester I had a new roommate. It was great because I felt free I was not inconvenience.

Not once, did I ask God how to handle that situation and as I reflect back, it was beginning to look like a pattern. It was as if God lived in Detroit not where I lived and as time went on my bond with God no longer existed.

Psalms I: 4-6 "The ungodly are not so: but are like the chaff which the wind driveth away. Therefore the ungodly shall not stand in the judgment, nor sinners in the congregation of the righteous. For the Lord knoweth the way of the righteous: but the way of the ungodly shall perish." kjv (unrighteousness)

It seemed like it happened overnight, I began to be involved in all kinds of things. I started drinking, drug usage not the hard stuff, not attending classes and gambling it was not a pretty site. All while I was performing these acts I would think about what if Jesus came back today would he accept me? But, that was a fleeting thought. I was still with my boyfriend in Detroit but I had some male friends at the University. I had become a hypocrite displaying qualities not befitting those of God and I knew he was not pleased because I felt that he no longer lived inside me. One morning I had awaken in my bed from partying all night. I could not move and suddenly my spirit removed itself from my body and drifted directly above me. I was looking directly at myself and in that moment I knew I was heading for a fall.

Pr 16:18 "Pride goeth before destruction, and an haughty spirit before a fall." kjv (fragility)

I prayed to God for help and I stopped drinking because in my mind it was detrimental to my health. I asked God to help me through this period in my life because I was not handling this situation properly. I could not help myself and there were many more things I did which were deployable. Attending a church would have been one way for structure but I did not have the mind set. I figured I would just stop doing some of the things or do them in moderation and God would accept that wouldn't he? When my sister, the stair step, one year under me, graduated from High School, she applied to my University, was accepted and we became roommates. My sister and I roomed together for one year before I applied to the University west of Detroit. This University was one of the ones I originally applied to and was accepted.

My brother was enrolled at this University, at this time, however he was transferring to a University east of his current University. I attended the University North of Detroit for two years. I participated in the following activities: I was a Dorm Resident Assistant, performed in several plays, help implement an experimental theater group, I wrote skits and acted on a show mobile, which toured the Southeast area of the State for one summer, I was on the University radio twice a week, I worked in the Dean's Office doing various duties and one year I assisted with the University's Freshmen Orientation program. Last but not the least a Pom-Pom girl for the Men's Basketball team.

As I arrived at my new University, my brother introduced me to his friends so I had individuals who could help me out. I was hoping that this move would put me back in good standing with God, however, I started out much the same way as I did at the old University. It is hard for me to admit but my first semester at the University I flunked out. I held the position that I knew more then the professors and told them so. One of my professor's, I had for two classes, when you looked at him you could see the racism printed on his face. He said to me in front of the entire class did I want to flunk his class I replied no and then he said well that is what it looks like to me so I am going to help you with that. He flunked me in one class and gave me a D in the other that put me on academic probation because my other grades were just as bad. Years later the same professor that tried to hinder my education applaused my talent with an exclamation mark. At the end of his lengthy accolade, he stated it looks like your attitude has changed. I did not address his negative remark because I did not want to stoop to his level of stupidity. Back to the present, I had to retreat and assess this situation, I was flunking out of College. I couldn't understand what was going on because I wasn't hanging out nor was I missing classes and then it hit me I just didn't like the atmosphere of this University. African Americans did not have a voice at this University and the City was the same. I just could not shake off this doom and gloom that had come over me. I felt the only way to get through this was to do what the majority of African slaves did when they were captured and ship to America. Those that survived assimilated themselves into the white man's world just to get by, so this is what I would have to do. I felt unlike myself, I was changing or turning into something dark created out of cruelty and hatred. I should have looked to God but I did not, maybe because my mind and heart was filled with revenge. Did I want to go to church? Well, the excuses I used were I could not walk to a church cause I did not have a vehicle. Stop it, this is just playing the pity game I had to come to the realization that I did not know how to get back into the grace of God. Then I started saying to myself he would not help me anyway I surely would not. Really, I could not face the fact that I was living outside of God's whelm.

I decided to talk to my brother about my academic probation and what role the Professor had played. He said I should have gone to the Dean of the University but it is a little too late for that now. Listen, he said, write a letter, to the Academic counselor explaining you had some type of hardship they might give you another chance. I wrote a letter, explaining my hardship, how I would achieve better grades. I was given a reprieve, and with that, I brought my grades up. With a mind set on revenge, I threw myself into every organization to assist African Americans dealing with the hypocrisy we faced coming from white America. I started working and going to school, I moved out of the dorms. I had a roommate again which did not work out and decided the best thing for me was to live alone. I decided to take a break from school because I needed a break it was too much pressure for me to deal with a full load of credits, working two jobs and trying to pay my rent. No longer enrolled in school, felt like a burden lifted off my shoulders. I still had plenty of friends who were attending the University but I did not hang out because I was working so much. I was working two jobs one at a burger joint another at a nursing home. I had no social life so I began to look for a job that would rake in the same earnings and free me up to party a little. I quit both jobs and started working at a restaurant 11pm to 7am. I figured with the tips I could afford to work one job. I still was not hanging out and felt like something was missing from my life. One night after looking at a religion movie, I sat down and had a talk with God. I said to God you told me I was your child well, where are you? I explained to him "I felt like I was struggling in all my areas in life, I needed help, please help me" I cried out.

Psalms 18:1-2 "I will love thee, O lord, my strength. The Lord is my rock, and my fortress, and my deliverer; my God, my strength, in whom I will trust; my buckler, and the horn of my salvation, and my high tower." kjv (deliverance)

The next night I went to work, I was the only African American that worked at this restaurant, and when African Americans came in to eat they were placed in my section. I knew the reason for this action African American did not leave tips. I started letting my customers know by telling them to leave a tip on the table when departing. In addition, I was quite funny so their experience was a great one. This night was slow, when three African Americans came in, one male and two females. Of course, they were seated in my section I approached them to take their orders. The male started by saying he would need plenty of water and one of the females said she wanted plenty of coffee. The second female continued to browse the menu. Later I discovered why she studies her menu. This female insisted upon editing the menu to get a meal she desired, which was not going to happen. The male suggested I place a pitcher of water on the table and as he ended, the first females said she would like a pot of coffee left at the table. I politely informed them that I could not bring them their desired items, however, their glass and cup would never go dry. Just one thing I would like you to keep in mind, I said, before you depart from this restaurant please leave a tip on the table, all three laughed out loud. That night was interesting because it was the highlight of my time working at that joint. They left a nice tip and something else, the male asked if I belonged to a church and if not would I mind coming to his church? I told him sure, I would. The females looked surprised and said this morning at 9am, in unison? Now it was I who was surprised I had not realized what day it was but I could not change my mind because my word had went forth. He informed me if I gave him my address and phone number he would pick me up, so I did with directions. Who gives someone their phone number and address without knowing them or someone they know knew them? Was I going crazy? No! I knew, when he asked me if I belonged to a church, at that moment the Holy Ghost within me leaped with joy, this was God answering my request. God heard me and answered my call I began to rejoice, because I was coming home with Gods blessing.

Psalms 18:1-2 "I will love thee, O lord, my strength. The Lord is my rock, and my fortress, and my deliverer; my God, my strength, in whom I will trust; my buckler, and the horn of my salvation, and my high tower. kjv (grace and mercy)

The next morning at 8am, I received a call from the male I met at the restaurant stating he would be at my apartment in 30 minutes. I would learn later that he was the Assistant Pastor of the Church. He arrived and off to the church we went a 30-minute drive from where I lived to a rural part of the township. The church was a small two story building on a short residential street however once inside it was larger then you had assumed. When you entered through the front door there was a staircase leading up to the sanctuary and two staircases one to your left and one to your right for access to the lower level. At the top of the stairs were double doors leading into the sanctuary, but before entering the sanctuary there was a door to your right with a sign saying Pastor Office, the left door lead to a coatroom. Entering the sanctuary there were metal chairs lined up on the right and left of the room with a center isle. The sanctuary sat about 100 + people. The pulpit had a long bench at the back and on the wall above was a crafted lit white cross. Then there are two doors on the pulpit, one on the left and one to your right. The door on the pulpit to the left lead to the sound and offering room, and the door to the right, lead to the lower level which also had a back-door entrance. The lower level consisted of: a kitchen, male and female restrooms, maintenance room, three large rooms used for classes and the outer area was the dining area seating about 100 + people. Underneath the front lower staircase was a storage room, which was filled with kitchen supplies. Overall, it was a lovely church and the members used it to its full capacity. I had started getting butterflies in my belly waiting to hear a word from the Lord. After Sunday school, I was introduced to the members present, and then I went into the sanctuary to await the Pastor's sermon. It was like music to my ears, he was talking directly to me. I could understand everything he said. In the Baptist church, I had attended, I never understood what the Pastor was talking about until he said, "if you don't give your life to Christ then you're going to hell. You must be baptized in the name of the Father, Son and the Holy Ghost before you can go to heaven." This would scare me and I would go up to the altar every time. I never came back to the service that night for the baptism, because my mother said, "First you should understand what is the meaning of being baptized." I thought not going to hell was good enough for me. After the Pastor's message, the congregation started praising the Lord dancing and calling out to Jesus then some fell to the floor and the Ushers would put a blanket over them. I knew then that this was

13

exactly like the church I had wandered into over 10 years ago. I started attending the church regularly, I felt accepted, so I joined. My Holy Ghost experience begins!

After attending the church for 6 months one of my friends called me wondering where I had been because we have had no communication. I informed my friend that I belonged to the Lord now and invited him to my church to experience what the Lord had given me. When the news had gotten out that I was now attending a church my friends felt like I had joined a cult. From all the things, they had seen me do and what they have known by witnessing others joining a church, they couldn't fathom the idea I had changed completely. They had known individuals joining a church and they did not change so something had to be wrong with this church. I tried to explain but I guess I could not reach them so I left them alone.

Mk 3:35 "For whosoever shall do the will of God, the same is my brother, and my sister, and mother." kjv (sanctify ones self)

At about this same time I realized the church was a closely knitted family not just in the spirit but also by blood. This is what people called a family Church. The Pastor and Assistant Pastor were brothers; District Missionary was the Pastor's mother; the Elder's and Deacon's were his cousins; Mother of the Church was an Aunt; and the Missionaries were Aunt's or Sister's to the Pastor. The congregation consisted of nieces, nephews and friends of the family, not related to the Pastor. It took me 6 months to discover this because I knew no one and did not ask. This was a spirit-filled, praising the lord praying for one another, speaking in tongues, prophesying church. The Assistant Pastor and the two females that came into the restaurant were siblings. I did not know that until maybe a month later after attending. I yearn to know more about the bible and whenever I read the bible and was confused, that Sunday during the Pastor's sermon or Wednesday during bible study, the Pastor would expound on my confusion. The Pastor could break down the word of God in such a way that you understood it and was enlighten by his preaching.

Matt 7:8 *"For everyone that asketh recieveth; AND HE THAT SEEKETH FINDETH; and to him that knocketh it shall be opened."* kjv (truth and belief)

I started going to Church whenever the doors were open, it felt good to be in a Church that had some direction and purpose. The Pastor implemented a witness program for all members to witness door to door throughout the city. The Church had been doing this program for some time but it was something new for me. The Church witness program grew and developed into a bus Ministry for Sunday School and Church services. I had a zeal for everything surrounding the word of the Lord, could not wait for a Church revival. A Revival strengthens your spiritual core, and I would become more alert of the devil's fiery darts. I attended this church for over 25 years and during that time my experience with the lord grew in knowledge, spiritual gifts and my personal life flourished in many ways. The Pastor's family and I were very close it was as if I became their little sister and I accepted this. I had asked, seeked, and prayed to the lord and he had provided.

Matt 7:8 *"For everyone that asketh receiveth; and he that seeketh findeth; AND TO HIM THAT KNOCKETH IT SHALL BE OPENED."* kjv (faith activated)

I was moving from job to job then finally God opened the doors of heaven and I received a position with the local City Government. At this time, my sister who was my roommate at the first University contacted me. She had gotten pregnant her first year at College, she finished her first semester and went home and had her baby that was a boy. She asked me if I would take care of her son, for a while, because her job had her travelling a lot she worked for the Federal Government. I told her yes and her son came to live with me. He was eight and I did not have a child that he could play with so, I went through procedures to become a Foster Mother. This would allow me to receive another child so he would have someone to play with. After receiving my certificate as a Foster Mother one of my friends said to me, "you should get this little boy that lives in my neighborhood." I told her it does not work that way. The next day the Foster Care Agency notified me about a young child whom happened to be the boy in my friend's neighborhood. In my 16+ years of being a Fostered Mother, the majority of children

I received were assigned to me by the announcement of someone saying, "you should get this child in my neighborhood". Immediately, this little boy, 10 years of age, became part of my family. Suddenly, my little sister was having difficulties with the law and I was the only one who could assist her by taking her two boys 4 and 5 years of age. God was bringing forth the dream I had. When I took my three nephews, I noticed they had a close bond so it was not a big deal to add one more to the crew. The saints started saying to me, you are doing too much, you are ruining your life by taking on responsibilities that are not your own, don't you want to get married? Who will take you with four boys? I informed them that this was God's doing not mine and he made me aware of this when I was just a child. So there was, no way I was not going to accept this duty, it was my destiny. The only thing my mother said was, as I went through the Fostering program, make sure I do right by these children and not do it for the money. You hear reports of people taken in foster children and treating them like their worthless. My kids cannot say that about me our relationship was tight and right. Majority of the children I fostered, were released to the care of their parents except the first young boy I received, he became my son. I had all my children call me Auntie because you do not have to be related to be an Aunt; you just have to love them. When my son asked me at the age of 12 if he could call me mom I said yes. I filed for adoption papers after his maternal mother said she would give up her rights only if I adopted him. She said this was the happiest she had ever seen him and he looked so good. She had come into town for a court procedure regarding him. The adoption was not processed until he was 19 years of age and I felt like it was too late to go through name changes so I sat down and had a discussion with him. We both agreed he would retain his last name but he will always be my son. I did not know that Children needs and wants are time consuming but I learned. No doubt, they needed me for stability but in some ways, I needed them for the same. My three nephews and son became a tight family, however, we had to overcome a few issues.

The Church ratio as it relates to members consisted of two males per female in adults as well as children. Therefore, the kids had friends immediately and the Pastor had four boys about the same ages as my boys so they became tight. I wanted my kids to have the same experience that I had when I grew up, so I moved into a mixed community where I thought everyone was treated with respect. However, time had changed and where I lived the people were racist. The kids got along fine until the parents got involved. I always remain neutral not involving myself in the neighborhood squabbles. A description, of my kids, starting with my son at the age of 10, he was short and very thin some would say frail looking. His body was under developed and he had poor co-ordination. He would walk into doors unable to stop himself no control over his motor skills. Also, a learning disability known as poor comprehension. I took him to the family doctor who sent him to a neurologist whom stated my son had some brain damage. Recommendation was Water Therapy, floating around in a pool on his back, which did not seem to solve his issues. I decided to seek the Lord who told me to purchase a bike for him to ride, so I did. That was an experience in itself but it worked along with additional assistance from the learning center at school my son over came his downfalls. My son was the oldest and he attended Junior high, my nephews Elementary and both schools were predominately caucasian students. The kids at my son's Junior High would push him around and call him names. I told him to tell the teacher's and they will take care of the matter. One day I noticed my son being very irritable so I asked him what was bothering him? He informed me that he was doing what I told him to do regarding the problems with the kids at school but the teacher's were not doing anything about it. I could feel his frustration and felt the only option was to allow him to defend himself. Therefore, I instructed him if they hit you, you hit them back. What I told him appeared to lift his spirit, but I hoped it would not surmise to a physical issue. Well it did, I received a call from the Principal the next afternoon informing me that my son had broken a boy's nose. I tried to listen to this Principal tell me the procedure that my son should have taken. I had told the same procedure to my son. I perceived this Principal was talking down to me so I interrupted him and said, when should an individual whom is following your procedure trying to work with the system, then finds out they are the only one following them? At what point should that person take matters into their own hand? My son was doing just what you've stated and no one helped to relieve him from his continual abuse of being victimized by the kids and your administration. Please let me know when a child should defend himself. The Principal was silent, I continued, when a parent identifies their child demeanor is brought on by a system that is suppose to be in control but actually is not. Rules and regulations are not being enforced, at any level, what should a parent do? My child looks at me as if to say can't you see what they are doing to me and what are you going to do? I have talked to the bus driver and my son teachers and they seem to notice nothing out of the way. A decision needed to be made on the behalf of my child, so I told my child if they hit you, you hit them back. Principal still silence, I then said, I guess now you want me to punish him, well that will not happen. What you need to do is inform the child and their parents that from this day forth my son will defend himself. Maybe that will eliminate some of the abuse and harsh attitudes from the kids, knowing that he will fight back. My son can only take so much and now I think the kids at the school will think twice before hitting him because the outcome will be the same. The Principal then said we cannot tolerate this attitude and I said well do something about it. I knew then it was time to move into the city. I turned to the Lord and asked him to find me a place that my children and I would feel safe.

The eldest nephew was 8yr old average height and built. I would say average because you could go into any store and purchase him clothes where as with my son it was a job. I never noticed any learning issue with him other then he had a problem of telling tall tales, he was a liar, and this I could relate. This caused problems, with him, being accepted with others, so, I sat him down to have a talk with him. I informed him that in order to have friends you must be honest and not make up stories that are not true. People should accept you for you not something made up, because once you fabricate you have to maintain that story. If, you do not, someone will find out the truth and then will not want to be your friend. In your case, this is what always happen. We are going to be moving soon and this will be your new beginning a fresh start telling the truth, he agreed.

My little sister kid's were adorable the youngest boy was 4, average built just like his cousin, buying clothes was not a problem, no learning issue just that he told all your business to any and everybody. This would frustrate me, but at least he was telling the truth, but it was not appropriate. Whatever happen to *"what's done at home stays at home,"* I guess this did not apply to him. I wanted him to understand that telling people's business was not nice, therefore I started telling everyone about the things he did right in front of him. Yes, I did, it may sound cruel but it was effective. He finally understood that his mistakes were private just like the foolish things that others do are private. They do not deserve to be re-enacted and told to the world. I remember when I was younger, I was at home with my mother one day when there was a knock at the door. My mother knew it was the insurance man so she told me to go to the door and tell him she was not at home. I opened the door and I told him that my mother told me to tell him she was not at home. He chuckled, and said, tell your mother I will be back next week then turned and walked away. My mother was so upset with me, and I did not understand why. When she received a phone call, she told them what I had done. Why didn't she just whip me, that would have been better then the humiliation of telling everyone what I had done? It taught me one thing, to listen to what my mother asked me to do, and ask questions if I did not have a good understanding. My little sister's oldest son was five a little teddy bear. He was as my son, trying to find him clothes, was a job. He had a learning disability and a thyroid problem, which I found out later in life. Once I got him the additional help at school, he was okay. Once he understood the lesson he excelled he also was kind always smiling and happy. However, by no means did I treat one better then the other they received the same measure of respect, care and love because they were all special to me. No, they were not angels, we had our share of issues, and one was coming to ahead. I sat them down to have a meeting of the minds to make sure we all was on the same page because they were causing problems with my babysitter, which were their teachers. Their primary goal of going to school first was to have a responsible adult watch over them while I am at work. Second and henceforth, learn to be attentive and participate with the teacher and classmates in their studies, do not become rebellious. Focus on academic achievement in math, english, history and the arts. An amicable agreement was made between them and me so that peace would rein in our home. At about this time my oldest brother called me to ask if he could come live with me, he needed a change from his environment, I told him yes.

At the beginning, it was stressful having my eldest brother living with us. My apartment was spacious for us five but with my brother it seemed crowded, lets say from having a little space to no space. It was a two-bedroom apartment, a small living room, a large eat-in kitchen with table, two large bedrooms and a small bathroom. There was no privacy for my brother because he slept in the living room on the hide abed. I knew at some point this was going to be a problem for him and might become stressful for the boys because my brother was an alcoholic. Once my brother became tipsy then came the name calling between him and the boys. When my brother got tired of playing this so called game he would turn evil and display anger toward the boys, and they didn't know how to deal with that. Finally, I decided to have a discussion with my brother about the atmosphere he had created since he moved in. I stated that in order for him to remain in this house he would have to stop drinking. I would help him find an institution that could assist him in this matter. Once successfully, off booze he would enroll in a GED course to acquire his high school diploma. I explained to him that by obtaining a GED it would allow him to get a job and then he could get away from the house, the boys and me for a while, and later get a place of his own. If he did not agree to this plan, we could not continue living together. I was hurting inside when I told him but ultimately it was his chose, he accepted the terms. I now had to deal with the name calling between the boys with him. My brother stated he was playing a game with the boys. I said a game! Well it is a nasty game, which ends badly. When I play a game with the boys its Monopoly, Sorry, Chinese Checkers, and Candy Land I then said, get the point. Name-calling is not a game it causes contention, strife and not permitted in this home. He agreed and completed all the demands successfully and I helped him find a place of his own. He lived with me 2 years and then moved out in an apartment with a friend.

One night, several months later, after my brother had moved out, one of my property owner's called me, she lived below me. She informed me that the boys had gotten into the garage and did some damage to her vehicle which they were restoring. She continued saying last week when the boys were playing with her cat they had tried to kill it, but the last straw was her vehicle, we would have to move. I woke the boys up, I was so angry, because just that weekend I noticed some paint on my son's coat and I asked them all what had they gotten into? I told them it would be best if they let me know now because if I find out later you will not be happy, and they were not. One thing about the boys they were not tattle tales, they would not tell where the paint came from. It seemed as if everything would be going great then something would happen negative and I would become frustrated. Nevertheless, as I look back never once did I say to myself I should not have taken on this responsibility. The next day I started looking for a place. I drove around looking for signs on houses or apartments to rent. I even called my last landlord because I had drove by the rental unit and noticed he no longer had his business below the apartment I once had rented. I thought maybe he had enlarged it and was putting it up for rent. Well, that is what actually happened and he had just rented the apartment. When I had started attending my Church, I would drive through an affluent area and I told God then I wanted to live in this area. I drove around in that area but I did not see a sign for rent so I reverted to the newspaper for units to rent when unexpectedly my property owner called. He told me I did not have to move because they have had no problems with me and my family, in the three years I lived there. The owner further stated, that kids will be kids, and he had told his daughter to put a lock on the garage door. I felt relieved but decided within myself that I would continue to look for a place. One day while looking through the rental ads in the paper I stumbled into the home purchase ads that had a home in the area where I had told God I wanted to live. Since it was not a rental, I continued looking. God said, ***"Go back, and call them."*** I called the owner and asked if they would consider renting the house? The owner, a female, said would you like to own a home? I said yes, but my finances are not up to par. She said, do not worry about that, set up an appointment with the realtor. I remembered a dream I had, it was my birthday and I was purchasing my home at the age of 30. I had previously discussed with God my desires in a home. It had to be a Cape Cod with 3 bedrooms, two bathrooms, a formal dinning room, a large kitchen, hard wood floors and if there was carpet it had to be brown, a basement, and just for a dare before viewing this house I added, the bathroom had to be green my favorite color. I don't know why I made all those demands but the bible says:

Jas 4:2 "Ye lust, and have not: ye kill, and desire to have, and cannot obtain: ye fight and war, yet ye have not, because ye ask not." kjv (revealed truth)

I set up the appointment with the realtor, the day after my birthday, he told me to meet him at the side rear entrance of the house. I did not drive by the house before my scheduled appointment I do not know why I just did not. Driving up to the house I noticed it was a Cape Cod and when walking to the rear door I saw the large fenced back yard, except on the east side of the property. When I entered through the side rear door, I stepped into the kitchen. It was a large kitchen with a large nook on one side of the room. Plenty of storage, a dishwasher, stove and refrigerator. I said to myself that is excellent, I would not need a kitchen table. We walked through the kitchen to the living room which had hard wood floors, a small foyer, when you enter through the front door, with a closet to your left for coats very small but nice. Then there was a door enclosing the staircase leading up stairs but on the other side of the first floor was a large dining room with brown carpet I said great again. I started to shake because everything I had asked for so far was present in this home. We started up the staircase that had brown carpet and at the top of the staircase, there was a large bedroom to your right and a small bedroom to your left, straight ahead was a full bathroom. This bathroom had a small shower, sink, toilet, linoleum floor and a door to your left behind it was a storage room. I ask if this was the only bathroom the realtor stated, oh I forgot to show you the one downstairs so we went back down stairs going through the dining room that led to the kitchen. Entering the kitchen from the dining room there were three doors, the door directly to your left was a large bedroom with a small closet. The door straight ahead from the dining room was the bathroom when I opened the door the entire apparel was green I almost screamed. The door to the right led to the basement, which had two sections. The right side was a sitting area partially paneled and the left side the laundry room and pantry area. This was my home it had every thing I ever wanted. The realtor took me into the kitchen and we sat at the kitchen nook and he said when would I like to move in, my reply was yesterday and he said so shall it be. I moved in 3 months later, with the help of the owners paying off my debts to acquire a mortgage from the most prestige's Mortgage firm in the City. This was truly a blessing from God.

***Matt 6:19-20** "Lay not up for yourselves treasures upon earth, where moth and rust doth corrupt, and where thieves break through and steal: But lay up for yourselves treasures in heaven, where neither moth not rust doth corrupt and where thieves do not break through nor steal." kjv (confirmation)*

Col 3:2 *"Set your affection on things above, and not things on the earth." kjv (faith)*

My brother and his roommate helped me move in. I felt good about this move because now the boys could participate in activities with a mixed racial group. The neighborhood I moved in was bi-racial to some extent more white then black but it was a step up from where we lived. Now everything was all right I got a part-time job and started furnishing my home. This job allowed me to cloth the boys with ease because I got a discount, but as in all things, it backfired. It seemed like I could not stop spending and before you knew it I was in debt over ten thousand dollars. I could not keep up with paying my current bills for trying to pay off the debt. I thought about filing a chapter 13 bankruptcy but after talking to an attorney, he told me to make arrangements and pay something on all of them or take out a second mortgage. I looked into getting a second mortgage, acquired one, and now I was sitting pretty, well let us say with ease. My main employment was becoming the source of my problem. An issue I will go into depth later.

The boys were thriving in the neighborhood there was a park at both ends of the street. Not only that but there were plenty of children living on the street. When I walked down the street or was in the grocery store, people would come up to me saying I had the most mannered children. Some neighbors had informed me that they were worried when I moved in because they had heard I was a Foster Mother. I guess being African American did not help much either, because I was not what they expected. I did not know what they expected but at the corner of the street was an Adult Foster home, they did not seem to have a problem with that. Twice a month I would take my boys out to eat and even then people would come by my table and tell me it is wonderful to see boys so polite and peaceful in a restaurant. It felt great to hear those encouraging words, and know it was their training, the love of God in their lives. One day a neighbor knocked on my door to tell me one of my nephews, my little sister's eldest son, who was chubby, had beat up his child that was half my nephew size. As I listened to him I kept saying to myself this does not sound like my nephew. I asked him was he sure? He said yes and wanted to know what I planned to do about it. I told me I would talk to my nephew and that this would never happen again. The neighbor seemed upset over my answer and yelled, "Well he is not welcome at my home ever again." I said I am sorry to hear that and I will inform him not to play with his son again or go to his house. I hope this satisfies you but this does not sound like my nephew it seems to me like this is a misunderstanding. Now I hope this is not the beginning of you being cruel to my nephews because I will not tolerate that action. I went on to say children fall out all the time and then they make up and are friends again. It's easy for them but for us we may never get to that point again. That is why, I do not interfere, in children matters however, I will become a referee. He then said, "Just keep him away from my home and child because I won't be so nice the next time." I did not say anything and when my nephew can home, I asked him what happened down the street with the neighbor's son? He said Auntie I do not know whom or what you are talking about what kid down the street. Therefore, I informed them all that they could not play with the neighbor's son or be around his house that way we would not have any problems with that family. I did not tell them about the neighbor coming to the house complaining. The reason for that is children feelings get hurt if someone expresses a negative action toward them especially when the child does not have an ideal about the situation. In addition, I felt whatever happen would come to light just wait and see. The following weekend I received another visit from the neighbor down the street, this time it was an apology and an explanation. He told me it was not my nephew who was fighting his child but my nephew who broke up the fight between his child and another child. The other child was bigger then the neighbors son so my nephew defended his child. He was so grateful to my nephew that he wanted all the boys to come down to his house. I accepted his apology and told him I would allow the boys to come down to his house. Then I said have a bless day. The neighbor turned slowly and walked away. I thought once again that their perception of an African American family was wrong.

The boys were enrolled in the neighborhood Baseball Little League. The League requirement was one parent had to work the refreshment stand at least once a month. I explained to them my work schedule prohibit me from participating, so they made an exception for me. The younger boys coach was an African American who knew my cousins and my brother. Their Coach was originally from West Virginia and that is my mother's place of birth. During the summers and around

Christmas time, when we were younger, our family would visit and we got to know people in the area. Although he knew my brother, I did not know him. I remembered one day I went to my nephews practice, and at that practice, their coach wanted me to participate. The coach wanted me to hit the ball, so that the boys could catch it and throw it to each other. In addition, I guess for a treat, he wanted me to run the bases when I hit the ball. I said okay, I was 235lbs, pudgy me, but beautiful. Ever since I've been a teenager my weight fluctuated which prompted one of my Aunts to say, if I didn't know you I would think you had some type of illness the way your weight differs each time I see you. At this time, I was not aware that I had a thyroid problem. There I was, standing at home base, with a bat in my hand, waiting for the ball to be pitched. The ball was pitched, I hit it and I threw my bat behind me and took off running. I went around first base, second base and as I approached third base, I heard panting behind me. I looked behind and there was the coach who was also about 200 pounds running directly behind me. I picked up my pace, made it around third base, and came into home safe. I was so out of breath I told the coach I am going to hang up my bat and throw away my ball. Please do not ask me to do that again, I could have had a heart attack. All of us were laughing, but really the coach and I was trying to catch our breath.

My son was in an older league, when I eventually went to his game I discovered that everyone disliked him, even the parents. My son did not meet their standards, he was not quite efficient in hitting the ball but when he did, he was a fast runner and great at stealing bases. It was tense for me when he came to bat the parents would be saying negative things loud enough that I could hear it. I would not say anything but prayed that he would do well. At the end of the summer, there would be an all star team game. The players pick the members to play on the all-star team. My son never made the cut so after two years I decided to enroll all the boys into the inter-city leagues. The boys enjoyed the inter-city leagues, and as I sat watching my youngest nephews basketball team play, I noticed, their coach let everyone play and they seem to be having a lot of fun. My son and older nephew were on the same team and their coach only allowed those he thought were the best players play. It appeared to me that their coach did not care for my son or nephew which this dislike extended and included me. This bothered me because when their coach looked at me it was with disdain.

However, I never vocalize my opinion regarding this matter to the boys or their coach. I knew, the coach, from my college days and did not have much to do with him. I never said anything negative about him but as I have learned, my name proceeds me. When their coach was absent from the game, there would be a substitute coach and that coach would let my son and nephew play. These substitute coaches were harsh with my boys, telling them to pick up the slack and perform the way they were instructed. These coaches also allowed my son and nephew to come out to their practice and taught them the principles of the game. The next year my boys had blossomed almost 2ft in height they were over 6ft and when they played it was something to behold. I have to say, they still had the same coach, but the coach now appreciative of their height and played them all the time. As a matter of fact, my boys took their team to the play offs and came in 2nd place. My son's ability to play went as far as the local Community College offering him a spot on their team. Requirements to play for the team were to register a full 12 credits per semester. My son would not have been successful in his grades by taking that many credits. My son continued to play in city tournaments winning trophies.

I tried to keep in touch with my brother, whom was living with his friend, but somehow I never contacted him. Then a friend told me my brother and his roommate was not getting along so, one day I went to my brother's apartment and knocked on the door. The door opened, I walked in and my brother was sitting on the floor in a bare apartment. I told him to collect his belongings then took him to my place. I gave my brother the smaller bedroom upstairs and moved all the boys into the larger bedroom. My brother had reverted to his old ways and that was not acceptable he agreed to clean himself up. Of course, the boys were glad to see him and did not argue over the arrangements. One day, while at work, I met a man who was in charge of hiring janitorial services for the educational system in the township. I inquired about employment for my brother and he informed me to have him come to the school and ask for him. My brother did and he was hired. Six months later, my brother brought a car and moved out to be closer to his employment. About this time, I was having difficulties with my vehicle and then finally no car at all. My sister steps in and gave me her car for a month. It was shortly after getting her vehicle I had a dream that I would meet this man and he would sell me a vehicle and let me pay for it on my terms. My brother informed me he knew a friend where he worked that was selling cars that students worked on. I set up an appointment at my home, to meet this man to look at the vehicle. The vehicle looked nice and he told me the vehicle was being sold for $600 and that I could make my own payment plan. I took my sister's car back to her and now I had a vehicle. I was enjoying my vehicle when I noticed there was a hole in the front floor panel on the passenger side. I did not know what I was going to do. One night while driving on the highway, coming back from a Church meeting out of town, God said, *"Look up"* and next to me was a truck full of Vans. God said, *"Which one do you want pick it out,"* I said I have never had a blue colored vehicle. To me a vehicle is a means of transportation, I am not into brand names. Then God said, *"Go down to the car dealer on Monday and get your Van."* I testified at Church what God said to me and I could hear the saints doubting what I said. That Monday from the dealer's, I drove out with a brand new blue Van the boys were excited and so was I. That blue Van lasted me over a decade before someone totaled the van.

Psalms 24:1-10 "The earth is the Lord's and the fullness thereof; the world and they that dwell therein. For he hath founded it upon the seas, and established it upon the floods. Who shall ascend into the hill of the Lord? Or who shall stand in his holy place? He that hath clean hands, and a pure heart; who hath not lifted up his soul unto vanity, nor sworn deceitfully. He shall receive the blessing from the Lord, and righteousness from the God of his salvation. This is the generation of them that seek him, that seek thy face, O Jacob, Selah. Lift up, your heads, o ye gates; and be ye lift up, ye everlasting doors; and the King of glory shall come in. Who is this King of glory? The Lord strong and mighty, the Lord mighty in battle. Lift up your heads, O ye gates; even lift them up, ye everlasting doors; and the King of glory shall come in. Who is this King of glory? The Lord of hosts; he is the King of glory, Selah." kjv (blessed assurance)

Now that I am reminiscing, I realized God has always been there taking care of me. It's like that poem where you see foot prints in the sand and in the end there is only one set of foot prints, and you ask where are you God and he say's, *"those footprints are mine, that's when I was carrying you."*

ROM 12:1-2 "I beseech you therefore, brethren, by the mercies of God, that ye present your bodies a living sacrifice, holy, acceptable unto God, which is your reasonable service. And be not conformed to this world: but be ye transformed by the renewing of your mind, that ye may prove what is that good, and acceptable and perfect will of God." kjv (letting go and let God)

At this time, I was lonely and wanted a companion. Everywhere I looked, there were couples and my desires had gotten out of control and had taken on a strong hold. The boys were teenagers and I felt like I deserved a little romance in my life.

Pro 18:22 Whoso findeth a wife findeth a good thing, and obtaineth favour of the lord." kjv (wait with faith)

This lesson was not a fruitful one for me because I was tired of waiting. The man I selected God had told me two years earlier that he was the one and I started running away from him because he was an alcoholic. However, what I had not done was listen to the full message. Once I heard, he was the one I said No! I closed my heart and ears. That sentence could have went like this: He was the one to stay away from; the one that will stray you in the wrong direction; the one that's lost and your involvement will only hinder you. WAIT! As in everything, it is all about me! I had made a decision, so what, I did not let God finish I went after him. It worked! We were an item, everyone in my sinful circle said we looked good together.

II Co 10:4 "(For the weapons of our warfare are not carnal, but mighty through God to the pulling down of strong holds;)" kjv (gluttony)

I did not know this at the time, but I had acquired a gluttonous spirit. Our image of gluttony is someone overweight, bound by overeating, but really, gluttony is the state of an individual who is obsessed with an object, person, place or thing. You are out of control. This glutton spirit had such a strong hold on me I could not break away. I could taste the desire that I desperately wanted, needed mounting inside me and I could not let go!

II Co 10:5-6 "Casting down imaginations, and every high thing that exalteth itself against the knowledge of God, and bringing into captivity every thought to the obedience of Christ; And having in a readiness to revenge all disobedience, when your obedience is fulfilled." kjv (God's self control)

I lost my way because of the decision I had made and then to make it worst I blamed it on the person I had chosen, for our relationship not surviving. When talking about this relationship I often made references of their issues not mine. I believed their need to live in the past was destroying their future and our companionship. Somewhere in their past, they had lost something precious and valuable and could not recapture it. In reality the fault was mine, because I had not weighed the cost of willingly leaving salvation to enter into a sinful state. I had convinced myself that something good could come from our relationship even if it was out of the realm of God's will. I was so out of it that I made excuses for my behavior. I would say to myself, I fell in love then I cared about this person. I learned from a Pastor that self-control was the opposite of gluttony and the way to become victorious was through Jesus. I could not continue to blame this person for my faults and judge this person because my expectations were not met. In my mind, judging this person made me feel like a saint. For getting, I too was going to be judged for the actions I took.

Rom 2: 1-3 "Therefore thou art inexcusable, O man, whosoever thou art that judgest: for where in thou judgest another, thou condemnest thyself; for thou that judgest doest the same things. But we are sure that the judgment of God is according to truth against them which commit such things. And thinkest thou this, O man, that judgest them which do such things, and doest the same, that thou shall escape the judgment of God?" kjv (blind)

Nevertheless, the relationship that never was, ended by me letting go and repenting from my sinful ways.

II Chr 7:14 "If my people which are called by my name, shall humble themselves, and pray, and seek my face and turn from their wicked ways; then will I hear from heaven, and will forgive their sin, and will heal their land." kjv (repentance good for the soul)

Once you sincerely repent, God will deliver you but it does not mean your adversary is going to give up. This demonic adversary will continue to torment you hoping to separate you from the love of God at any cost. Therefore, the fiery darts of the adversary begins. I sought the word of the Lord, and he prepared me for what was to come in a dream. The dream began with me not working for the City Government. I felt lost but not broken, somehow, it appeared like there was hope, and I was talking to a co-worker. I woke up from the dream nervous and went to work feeling unease. The next night the dream continued I was back at work and the co-worker whom I was talking to in my first dream was no longer working for the City Government. In the dream I kept asking everyone where was this co-worker, but no one seem to acknowledge me. I was confused and seemed misplaced I continued looking around. I noticed we were at a banquet for someone but I did not know whom and then I woke up. The next day I told this co-worker, I had a dream about him. I told him the dream and explained that my dreams come true. This co-worker, Union President, just looked at me and smiled as if to say it is just a dream. The next day I was fired.

This was not the first time I was fired from this organization but it was the first time I knew it was going to happen. It did not surprise anyone that I was fired because my employment was tumultuous and I was known as an infamous individual in this organization. When you are an employee in Government organizations, you are governed by Labor Laws, which are handled by Union Representatives. At this time, I happened to be the Union Grievance Chairperson, a good one. It was my job to ensure individuals were not displaced or fired unjustifiably. In fact, it was my job to ensure their employment regardless of their own demise. A win-win situation was instrumental in what I considered my strategy in negotiating ones employment. My first time being terminated by this organization was when I was a Union Steward. Management was trying to terminate me for poor workmanship, because I was a thorn in their side. If they could find some inaccuracy in my workmanship, they could develop a paper trail of wrong doings leading up to a reprimand and eventually termination of employment. In the end, they did not have to because my attitude gave them the rights to terminate me. Management allowed a co-worker, when I was out on leave, to go through my workload looking for discrepancies once found a reprimand was issued. Once I returned to work, I would be questioned concerning the discrepancy and then I would counteract their findings by producing when and by whom the inaccuracy was generated and the reprimand would be removed from my file. Management could not create an on going list of poor workmanship so they attacked my work performance with co-workers. I then would have to justify the co-workers and myself. One day after coming back from vacation my desk was a mess. This was a usual harassment, but this time I did not hold my peace and when management asked me to come into their office I said no because my appointments were beginning in 30 minutes. The employee, who I had dreamt about was, the Union Grievance Chairperson, at this time, asked me if I wanted him to come in my Supervisor's office with me, I said no. I was fired due to insubordination. At the time, the organization was going through a hierarchy change and the new Assistant Manager in my defense stepped up and stated, *"No we will not fire her for this mistake, she has been an excellent employee for 15 years. Her reprimand will be a two week suspension without pay."* Management had successfully done what they sought out to accomplish I was no longer a Union Representative due to my suspension. I no longer was in good standing with the organization, one of the requirements in order to hold this position.

My life, in the present, seem like it was falling apart again and it had started to affect my demeanor not so much outward but inward. Anytime someone mentioned work related matters I would become intolerable even to myself but I couldn't stop myself and to top it off once again I was, a Union Representative, the Grievance Chairperson. I had begun driving around not aware of where I was or where I was headed. I would continue to drive until the area became familiar and then hopefully remember where I was headed. Then one day I came into work and did not know where I was or why I was there, I realized it was time to see a physician. I was making myself miserable over Management new ploy, The Reduction In Government Work Force. I was so concerned about employee's job security that I had not noticed my health issues. In fact, the co-worker, I dreamt about, now Union President, he and I met with management, to discuss methods to put the employees at ease, while management implemented the program. The suggestions we made management agreed and immediately put them into effect. Meetings were scheduled throughout the organization so employees could ask questions regarding their concerns relating to this work force reduction. All employees in my work area were gathering in the organization board auditorium, for the meeting. Management opened up discussing the process they were going to take. When Management had finished they opened it up for questions. One employee known for making suggestions stood up and started giving solutions to many of the outlines Management had just discussed. I stood up, interrupted him, and reminded everyone that there are procedures in place for those suggestions. Due to time constraints, we needed to move forward. This meeting was being conducted by the organization Head Manager, same individual that defended me in my first termination. He stated I was right about procedures in place for employee's suggestions and went to the next couple of individuals, which I was one of them. When it was my turn, I asked a question that everyone wanted to know but did not ask and the head of Management could not answer it. The Assistant Manager had answered that question, for me, in a meeting we had earlier that week. I had already informed the employees in my work area that this question would be discussed. I was aghast! I made the head Manager aware of what his assistant had informed me. Furthermore, this serious matter needs to be addressed. Head Manager then dismissed the meeting and everyone went home on time. The following Friday my Supervisor called me into the office and informed me that a meeting had been scheduled for us to meet with the Head Manager at the end of the day. I asked my Union President, the one I dreamt about, was he aware of this meeting, he stated he knew nothing, so I went down to the meeting alone. Present at this meeting was the Head Manager, my Supervisor and I. The Head Manager informed me that he did not like the way I conducted myself at the meeting the other day. Furthermore, if I interrupted anyone or if he became aware that I had interrupted any one for any reason I would be fired. Then he asked, "Do you understand?" I said no! Manager replied looking directly at me "what don't you understand?" I said, any of it. Then the Manager stood up and left the room. When he returned, he stated Human Resources informed him that a Union Representative should have been present and that one was coming. I knew that this meeting was not going to end in a written reprimand or termination because my Union President had to be notified of such a meeting and representation had to be present. Normally it would have been me, Union Grievance Chairperson with Union Steward to discuss the actions that Management was taking. A Union Representative entered and Head Manager made that same statement regarding interrupting individuals and if I understood and I said no. The Head Manager then stood up and in a loud voice said you are fired and then stormed out leaving my Supervisor, Union Representative and myself sitting in the room. Thirty seconds later, my Supervisor exited, my Union Representative looked at me and said **"What do we do now?"** and I said we fight. I was not trying to be brave or strong I was stunned. I did not have time to think I just knew I was fired unjustifiably. At the time, I was trying to wrap my head around not having any money to pay my mortgage, two car notes, credit card debts and utilities. I did not know how I was going to survive. My first step was to seek assistance from somewhere so I sought General Assistance, which was to no avail. They informed me that I would have to sell my home, vehicles and anything of value before they could assist me. Those items were considered assets that prevented me from acquiring any assistance from their organization. I filed for unemployment, was notified that my employer denied my request, so I decided to fight the denial. When I went to the unemployment office to file against the denial the unemployment Agent looked at me as if I deserved to be fired. No doubt, this agent had read what my employer had documented for refusal of benefits. Suddenly as I was explaining my case, the Agent's countenance changed and then I said I have it documented because my Union is filing a Grievance. The Agent said let me look at it. The Agent read it and informed me at that moment that I will receive my unemployment benefits tears came to my eyes. I felt like this was the beginning of my battle for survival. My life was now in the mist of an avalanche but God has taken the rein.

Ps 37:25 I have been young and now am old; yet have I not seen the righteous forsaken, nor his seed begging bread." kjv (you are not along)

Two Grievances were filed Regional and State - Labor Board. Management wanted me to clean out my desk and take my pension, which I refused to do because I knew I was coming back. If I had taken my pension and used it I might not have been able to repay it when reinstated. Management might not let me reactivate my status, original employment starting date due to the termination. The Union Attorney approached me with an offer from Management, which stated, "if I considered counseling for my actions they would give me probation."

I told the Union Attorney I would think about it and call him back. I then called my sister, the one I roomed with in College, and told her about my termination and Management's offer. My sister had been an infamous Union Representative at her place of employment. She said do not fall for that offer! It is just a ploy, if you accept that deal management will use it against you should they deem your action were similar at a later time, then terminate you. You tell them you will go to counseling if the Manager also attends counseling. When I told this to the Union Attorney, he just started laughing, and then said, you are something else. Then all of a sudden, it started raining doom and gloom.

My sister who roomed with me in College her son was in a car accident. My nephew was living with my brother because he needed a firmer hand. He was doing well but when he was not working, he would drive up to visit his cousins. I saw my nephew the night of the accident, I told him before anything bad happens please go home. That night my nephew was in a car accident. There were several individuals in the vehicle with him and everyone walked away but him. In the end, my nephew became a quadriplegic and still is to this day. My other nephews decided they wanted to go home and their mother retrieved them. One year later, they both graduated from high school and had a dispute over a young lady. I had allowed my younger nephew to come back to live with me so he could attend College. As quiet as it was kept I told them both they could come back but the older brother did not want to if the younger one was there. Five years later the youngest nephew is married, has four sons, one daughter and is a Police Officer. He is deeply in love with the Lord and involved in his church with his family. His brother died from Graves disease in that five year lapse, he was over 400lbs. My mother called me the day he died and told me he was in the hospital and it was serious. I was getting ready to come home when he passed away. At the funeral, every one was hurting he died from thyroid complication. My brother whom had been living with me off and on had come back to live with me. He had, had an alcoholic relapse. I felt responsible for my brother's relapse because the person I was dealing with was also an alcoholic. My son had enlisted in the Navy, which I tried to stop him, but it did not work. He served for two years came home got a job and is doing fine.

II Pe 3:9 *"The Lord is not slack concerning his promise as some men count slackness; but is longsuffering to us-ward, not willing that any should perish, but that all should come to repentance." kjv (God's word)*

During the Regional Grievance hearing, my Supervisor informed the Arbitrator that she was unaware of what was going on and quite shocked when I was fired. This was true and I admired my Supervisor for stating that fact. Following the Regional hearing, we had the State Labor Board hearing. After one hour into the meeting I went into the restroom, there was a large mirror I saw myself and was shocked at my appearance. I looked sick, my clothes hung off me making them look oversized. After the hearing I felt like I had a good chance of winning my case. Suddenly, I started receiving money packages from my fellow co-workers. I was astonished, because each time I ran out of money I would get a package from somewhere or someone. I applied for several part time positions and gained employment. One was with the Public School working with Autistic children administering learning skills. It was a rewarding job and I enjoyed it, but shortly thereafter funding for the internship program was depleted. Some of the interns needed this placement to complete their course. I knew I would be going back to my place of employment soon so I terminated my position hoping this would allow continued funding for some of the girls to complete their semester. That same week I received an invitation to a retirement party. It was for the Union President the one I dreamt about and told him about my dream. I remembered telling him that he would not be working at the organization when I returned. I realized, from the dream, this was the banquet, his retirement party. I also knew that this was a confirmation that I would be returning to my job.

Doing this time my Pastor became ill unto death. I had shut my eyes to what was going on around me. I was barely going to Church but I tried to keep up with what was happening. When the news came to me that the Pastor was ill I called him, which happened to be the day he was admitted into the hospital. He kept repeating my name until I said I would see you at the hospital. My Pastor was born with a genetic disease and was occasionally sick but always overcame his illnesses. I just assumed he would overcome this setback. The Pastor was admitted in the hospital and I could not bring myself to visit him, as I have done in the past, because I was in a sinful state. When he passed away, I was devastated. He was like a brother to me and I did not give him the time of day at the end of his life. I almost did not go to my Pastor's funeral but I did, however, I did not stay for the repast because I was so distraught. I cried for days and prayed for forgiveness it seemed like I was walking around in a daze. I was spiraling fast downward after my Pastor's death. I had stopped going to church completely and heard that they were going through a reconstruction in leadership. I felt like I was in hell, then a knock at the door it was my Assistant Pastor. He told me the Lord had sent him to my house to give me his last 30 dollars. Money had become scarce and every cent I had went toward my mortgage. It was a blessing I did not have a car note it was paid in full the month before my termination. The pantry was dry and I did not know where my next meal was coming from. His money would have been a blessing unto me, but I told him I could not take his money. He then said, "So I don't get my blessing?" I took his money, thanked him, and told him I would be coming to Church. The next day I received my Income Tax it arrived right on time. It lasted 3 months and I still had not heard a word regarding my Grievances. Once again, my money had run its course and I did not know how I was going to pay my mortgage the next month. The next day I was in my backyard, painting my shades for my living and dining room windows, when I received a call from my Union Attorney whom informed me that I had won both of my cases the Regional and State Labor Law. The Union Attorney said that I would be re-instated, with back pay and that I should report to work the day after the holiday. I thanked the Union Attorney, put away my painting equipment, went into my bedroom shut my door and began to cry.

Ps 37:32-33 *"The wicked watcheth the righteous, and seeketh to slay him. The lord will not leave him in his hand, nor condemn him when he is judged." kjv (not forsaken)*

I had heard that the Head Manager wanted to contest the ruling from the Regional Arbitrator and the State Judge Labor Laws, but the City Commission voted against him. I was shaking all over and praising God for his **Grace and Mercy.**

Ps 37:34 "Wait on the Lord, and keep his way, and he shall exalt thee to inherit the land: when the wicked are cut off, thou shall see it." kjv (stay in God's will)

It had been a total of nine months before I was reinstated to my same position, with back pay. Of course, I no longer was the Grievance Chairperson but I knew at this time it was better to be seen and not heard. This would be my motto upon my return.

Returning to work caused a domino effect with the co-worker currently occupying my position. The individual preforming my job had to return to their job and pay status and the person performing in their job had to return to their job and pay status. Luckily, it only affected the two individuals that worked in my department, but unsettled feelings existed due to this undertaken. The co-worker that performed my job now had an attitude. Our relationship was satisfactory up until this happened and now this co-worker felt that all my opinions, that I have stated, involving our organization were false and misleading. This co-worker stated I always think everything negative that has occurred at my employment was brought about by Management because they were making a statement, "Do not interfere with the powers that be." She felt, I thought everything was centered on me it was all about me. I knew I had to diffuse this behavior before it started spreading through out the office. This co-worker was a saint of God and now she was being manipulated by a negative spirit. I continued to keep a positive attitude not bringing any hostility towards this co-worker over her comments and then I had a dream. God showed me that the City was going to eliminate the program I administered and the other two co-workers and I would have to bump or move into an existing position. The dream indicated that my co-workers would be placed into positions, in the organization, however I would not at the close of the program. I went to both co-workers and told them my dream they just looked at me. Previously I had informed them about other dreams so their reaction was not one of unbelief. Shortly thereafter, we were informed that our program was being terminated. When the co-worker, who had been performing my job, obtained a new position, she came to me and said, "you were right, it has been all about you." I just smiled and told this co-worker do not worry everything is going to work out fine. On my birthday, this co-worker gave me a bronze paperweight with the inscription written, *"IT'S ALL ABOUT ME".*

At this time, I was back at church where now the Assistant Pastor was trying to continue the spiritual obligations that his brother had maintained but couldn't. His sister's didn't want him in that position. It is something when you allow a demonic spirit to interfere in the work of the Lord. The sisters approached me regarding their concerns wanting me to side with them. I informed them that their brother our deceased Pastor wanted his brother in his place and that they were going against his wishes and against Gods anointed one.

1Ch 16:22 *"Saying, Touch not mine anointed, and do my prophets no harm." kjv*

In the end, the Assistant Pastor left the church and I went with him, we formed a new church. I was under his leadership for 18 months and then he passed away. I was so hurt and went through a guilt trip again becoming irrational, believing I had caused this to come upon him. His death was caused by an enlarged heart or complication of the heart. I was once again distraught then several of his sisters' approached me and apologized for their behavior toward their brother. This was related to the struggle of accepting him as Pastor of the church. I felt it never was up to me to accept their apology just make it right with God. Now, I did not have a church to attend and I used to think what does a person do on Sunday if they do not go to church? Well, I discovered, you stay in bed, go to the grocery store, clean your home or watch television. Everything was changing and I could not see myself attending any church. I was unstable mentally at work mainly when it came to communicating with Management. If I had to respond to a work related issue or was asked a question by Management I would hesitate before speaking. Then when I spoke, I would stutter then slowly I would have an anxiety attack. I had discovered that due to my termination I had developed a lack of confidence and feared another loss in employment should I say the wrong thing.

It seemed sudden, I was at the close of the program. My co-workers had been placed in a secured position within the organization. I received accolades from my Supervisor for the way I performed the closing of the program especially my attitude. I accepted my supervisors praise keeping in mind it was best to be seen and not heard. Being an employee working 40 hrs a week, you learn that the majority of your time is spent with your co-workers. Your life and the lives of your co-worker are engulfed together and you began to know aspects of their lives and vice versa. It is in that time you have the ability to display your Godly virtues and influence those around you about the love of God. God does not want you to be quiet and hide like a mouse. God demands that you present your body as a living sacrifice of his word.

Co 3:22-24 "Servants, obey in all things your masters according to the flesh; not with eye service, as men pleasers; but in singleness of heart, fearing God: And whatsoever ye do, do it heartily, as to the Lord, and not unto men; Knowing that of the Lord ye shall receive the reward of the inheritance: for ye serve the Lord Christ." kjv (witness for Jesus)

With the program dissolved, now I could concentrate on open positions available or bump into a position within the organization. The bumping process had changed, I would be allowed two bumps as opposed to many. After making my selection a test would be administered, and if I failed the test, the process would began again. If I failed a test twice in trying to secure a position I would be placed on laid off mode until a position with my qualifications became available. However if I choose a position and Management felt I was not qualified, no test would be administered to determine eligibility. The process would continue until I found a position, which had Management approval. After one month of searching for a position, I received a letter from Management stating I was not qualified for any position currently open. There was talk that I would be placed on laid off mode but then Management decided to use me as an Employee Floater. An Employee Floater is one that assumes a position that needs to be performed due to the following; an employee was on a leave of absence; sickness or family matters; maternity leave; or positions that Management had not planned to refill but still needed assistance. I was in this position for 9 months and during that time, I successfully completed each job requirement. One problem, with being a Floater, was that, each job duties I performed my wage would drop to that job pay scale. Havoc was the name of my financial affairs, due to my continuous change in my salary. Finally, a position became available that Management felt I was qualified to perform. Testing for the position was waived if I accepted the position, if I rejected the position, I would be laid off. The position was one I occupied 20 years ago when I was initially hired into the organization. The pay scale for this position was six steps below my normal pay scale. I accepted the position because I felt management was pressuring and threatening me at the same time. When I received my first check, in my new position I went into the women restroom and cried. I did not know how I was going to survive and then I remembered my Father will supply all my needs according to his riches and glory, knowing this I felt better. After working in this position for 4 months the pay difference did not seem to bother me and then my new Supervisor called me into her office regarding some training. The Supervisor said to me *"you are not what I expected? I mean, what I had heard was that you were a difficult individual to work with and you really aren't."* My response was that Management could not separate the Union Representative from the City employee.

One day one of my Pastor sisters reached out to me and asked what church was I attending, when I informed her I was not. She said, "You should be attending somewhere because you need a covering." A covering is a Pastor whom prays for you and if you should die, administers your funeral. She continued to say if you haven't decided where to attend why don't you pay your tithes to my church until you make your decision better yet, why don't you attend the church I'm going to. I have always paid my tithes, so I did give her my tithes and in the end started attending the church and became a member. I really did not want to attend another family church because of my last experience and now this church was a family church. I often wondered if Jesus had a problem with his family because several disciples were related to him. The church I now attend is a family church and was a relative of my belated Pastors. In fact, favored them in appearance and behavior. I would leave the church crying because I saw my deceased Pastor every time I came to church. After attending the church for a while, I got over my initial reaction. I attended this church for 2 yrs and then the Pastor closed the doors because he felt the need to join another church. He expressed his desire and asked the membership to join him as he made this move. The membership did not want to attend his choice. My Pastor then resigned his duties to the church, and then gave it to his cousin. I started floating around looking for a church to meet my needs. I eventually ended up attending my last church. It was the same building but different leadership. I attended this church for 3 yrs before I moved out of state.

My mother decided to build a home out of state, south of Detroit, taking my father who had dementia and my quadriplegic nephew with her. I looked into assistance for my mother because she was in her late 70's. In addition, my sister and I had begun driving to my mother's house every other weekend to help her out. The trip was an ordeal, first I had to pick up my sister, who lived 2 hours from me, then drive 3 hours to my mother's place. My sister does not drive, she cannot obtain a drivers license, due to drunk drinking charges, and to this day, she cannot acquire a drivers license. I performed this task for 3 years until I retired. In those 3 years, my father past away and my sister retired and moved in with my mother helping to take care of her son. I still came down every other weekend because prior to my father's death I would take care of him on those weekends. I had not realized what my mother was going through until I had to follow my dad around, you had to watch him like a hawk. Sometimes, maybe I should say the majority of the time, my father would forget who I was and would say to me if I asked him to do something "yes ma'am or no ma'am." Those times were so cute and endearing, however, there were times he would let me know who he was and became difficult to handle. Overall, it was delightful to take care of my father for the short period. It's true the older you get you mentally and physically revert back to a child and it was in those moments I felt sad, cause he didn't know who I was, and the love I've always had for him.

At work, my motto was in place being seen not heard. Many employees would call me to assist them with Union issues and depending on my relationship with them I would tell some what to do and others I would inform them to go through their Union Representative and have that steward contact me. I was trying to keep a low profile so Management would not have a cause to attack me. It had been 2 yrs since I had been in this low paying position when I saw a job position in another city. I applied for the position had an interview, which was successful and I was selected for the position. This new position was the same one I held at the city before my program was terminated, however, it's pay wage was less then what I originally received from the city. When I was offered the job, I informed them that I needed more revenue, in order to accept this position. I gave them my preferred starting wage and a week later, I received a call declining my offer but letting me know the offer remained on the position. I sadly declined the position. It was at that moment I realized I had the ability to successfully apply for a position, be chosen outside of my organization, why could I not do the same in this organization? It was time to engage with Management and reactivate my bumping rights.

First, I had to develop some confidence that had vanished after my second termination. Secondly, I had to find a position, hopefully with the same pay scale I had been demoted from, that I could bump into with Management's approval. I selected a position, Management felt I did not qualify, however they allowed me to test for it. Of course, they did inform me that this would be one of my bumping options and should I fail the test I would have one remaining. A test was administered and thanks to the glory of God, I passed. The test was not simple it was rigged. The test consists of about 10 mathematical problems and general questions. The test also gave a brief synopsis as to how you should derive to the correct answer, but one-step was left out. I am known for reading too much into a question and I could not figure these out. If I did the problem long form, I did not come up with the same result short form. Then God pointed out there was a step missing. I pointed this error out to the individual administering the test who was quite apologetic. The person administering the test left the room, I had written my answers both ways. When the person returned, I was informed a step was missing and that I had passed the test.

Psalm 13:1-6 "How long wilt thou forget me, O Lord? Forever? How long wilt thou hide thy face from me? How long shall I take counsel in my soul, having sorrow in my heart daily? How long shall mine enemy be exalted over me? Consider and hear me, O Lord my God: lighten mine eyes; lest I sleep the sleep of death; Lest mine enemy say, I have prevailed against him; and those that trouble me rejoice when I am moved. But I have trusted in thy mercy; my heart shall rejoice in thy salvation. I will sing unto the Lord, because he hath dealt bountifully with me." kjv (recovery)

I was back to my previous pay scale, a six-step promotion, due to the bump. I got along great with my new Supervisor who after a month left due to accepting a position outside of the organization. My next Supervisor was the Assistant Director of the Division. He became my Supervisor because I was told they were looking for someone who could handle me. Finally, my next Supervisor was a co-worker I had worked with in my old department that had closed. We worked well together and this Supervisor let me in on everything that Management was trying to do against me because once again I was the Grievance Chairperson.

Now that my mother had moved out of state, I needed to find a church to attend. My mother was originally of the Apostolic faith later she let me know her faith was African Methodist Episcopal AME, where as I was, COGIC - Church Of God in Christ. I goggled to find a COGIC and found one 14 miles from where we lived. I attended it but I did not feel a vibe so the next Sunday I decided to go to another COGIC in that neighborhood. I was on vacation and thought this was a good time to find a church. As I was driving to another location, I got lost and when I finally found the church no one was present. I decided to go to another church in the area, and no one was present at that church. Now I was frustrated and decided to go back to the first church I attended last Sunday and got lost. Yes, I had, a GPS that needed to be updated, because it was always reconfigure rating, which was nerve wrecking. I was talking to God and I was saying Lord all I want to do is find a COGIC why is I having such a difficult time. I am lost, just driving around and then God pointed out to me, *"look to your right,"* and I would look and he would say, *"There's my church,"* and there was a church; and then he would say *"look to your left"* and I would look and he would say, *"There's my Church,"* and there was a church. Each time God told me to look to my left or right he would say, ***"THERE'S MY CHURCH."*** God was letting me know that COGIC does not define him, wherever his word is being preached is his church. I began to cry and when I looked up, I was at the first church I had attended. I went into the building rejoicing in the word of God. The next time I came home my mother asked was I looking for a church that we both could attend and I had said sure. My mother and I started visiting various churches until one day she had spotted a church across the road and told me about it so I decided to investigate. I discovered it was a church but its name was not on the building neither was the time of services. One day, I saw cars around the building and decided to find out what was going on. I talked to a young woman that was present in the building that gave me the name of the church and the times of service. That Sunday my mother and I attended. The building was a large industrial building with a large sanctuary and many rooms, which later I would learn, were classrooms. This church was a Non-denominational Church derived from a Baptist origin. Its ethnicity was predominately Caucasian and it had two services both mornings, one early and one late morning session. The children had there own classes and services and were not included in the adult session unless there was a special program involving them, then it would be announced and preformed in front of the assembly. My mother enjoyed the service and so did I and soon we became regular attendees.

A Union Representative presented an opportunity for me to become the Grievance Chairperson again should I accept. They stated that they had talked to numerous employee's whom had declined however if I ran they would vote for me. Many employees did not want to hold this title because of the hardship it places on an employee. I told them I had to think about this before making my decision. I had to count the cost of occupying this position because of what had happened when I held it previously. When I held the position of Grievance Chair person my behavior and attitude was flawed. I felt entitled in the position it belonged to me because I excelled in it. I can define myself as being prideful with a haughty spirit and a superior attitude that I was better then everyone and could do anything and then I fell.

Pr 16: 19-25 "Better it is to be of an humble spirit with the lowly, than to divide the spoil with the proud. He that handleth a matter wisely shall find good: and whoso trusteth in the Lord, happy is he. The wise in heart shall be called prudent: and the sweetness of the lips increaseth learning. Understanding is a wellspring of life unto him that hath it: but the instruction of fools is folly. The heart of the wise teaches his mouth, and addeth learning to his lips. Pleasant words are as an honeycomb, sweet to the soul, and health to the bones. There is a way that seemeth right unto a man, but the end thereof are the ways of death." kjv (lean unto the Lord)

I sought the Lord on whether to obtain this position. What I did not want to happen is what occurred each time I occupied the position. In addition, I had learned being in God's will is the best decision I could make. God told me to place my name on the selection list for the position, however I would not campaign for the position. The election was held and I became the new Grievance Chairperson but I kept a low profile. I handled cases that the Union felt was against our contract and cases between employee's and Management only when I was requested by Union Stewards.

I have had a peaceful employment for five years and now my current Supervisor planned to retire. My Supervisor did not want a party and was a little upset with Management as it relates to his retirement. My Supervisor left one day from work and never returned. Now, that is saying something. I believe it was planned because we said our goodbye a week earlier. My Supervisor did inform me to continue to perform my job duties above board and to watch my back. I had three more years left before I retired and two years remaining as Grievance Chairperson. When my Supervisor left, Management selected three exempt employee's as my Supervisors. This procedure reminded me of my previous city position, which was terminated after I had been reinstated. I had a caseload of over three hundred files, when the city returned it to the state, the state divided it into three new positions. Management decides to put three Supervisors over me and I did not know whom to address first, and no one ever told me. My department consisted of a staff of five, which included me, and three of them were my Supervisors. My office space was a small cubicle that was shared with another part-time employee during the summer months. Then Management decided to reorganize our office space and I received an office of my own. No longer was I sitting in the breezeway where individuals walked back and forth in front of my office..... Oh yeah, I was the only one sitting out there, everyone else had an office. Now, I had an office, I could not believe it, I guess they did not see that one coming. I had my office for eighteen months then my beloved Supervisor retired. Management decided to give me three Supervisors and moved the department to the front of the building. Once again I was in a breezeway and everyone else had an office. We were there for about three months and then we moved upstairs and this time my office space was an embarrassment. My office was outside every ones office in between the file cabinets and in front of the office coffee station where everyone congregated. It may have been all in my head but sometimes I could hear sniggering from my co-workers. My desk faces a wall so I could not look directly at them.

Jam 1:19-20 "Wherefore, my beloved brethren, let every man be swift to hear, slow to speak, slow to wrath: For the wrath of man worketh not the righteousness of God." kjv (adhere to God's word)

I needed much prayer during that time. Some of my friends, co-workers, would come over to see exactly what I had been talking about then say you were not lying. That was okay, but what really got me was the noise my co-workers would keep up around my workstation. Sometimes I would shut their doors, but then I decided, that action only made them aware of my irritation so I stopped doing that. The best solution for this matter was to act as if I wasn't bothered but all the while I was burning up inside. Management only wanted to know what I was up to and hoping to catch me performing Union duties during working hours. No, I did not perform Union duties at work and made sure employees called me when I was out in the field on my cell phone, or met me at lunch. Of course, Union appointments had to be excused by my Supervisors, which was not a problem. I just scheduled my work appointments around them. One thing Management couldn't do and that was find a fault in my work performance and this time I didn't work with another employee, so no false allegations could be brought against me. Problems arose at work with the new implementation of The Reduction In Divisions-throughout the organization. This was not a good time to be employed with this organization because once again the organization was restructuring the work force.

Management had begun demoting and eliminating African American positions and promoting Caucasian employees. Management was reducing the work force in certain areas and eliminating departments, or employee positions. This would not have been a problem if they conducted it according to our Contract Agreement. The Contract stated that when reducing the work force in an area you must eliminate the least seniority employee first especially if the position in question has several employees performing the same or similar task. What Management executed was eliminating individuals with the most seniority and leaving the one with the least in their place. This prejudice was tearing the work force apart and all the African Americans were feeling the sting. The Union felt this was a fight to undertake through the Grievance Chairperson. African American employees did not want to grieve against management in fear of retaliation. Yes, even though their jobs were the ones being eliminated. On top of that, they could not find another position in their pay scale. This meant demotion in pay by accepting a lesser job title, if one existed, that they could bump into. This put me in an uncompromising position with Union employees because Caucasian Employees felt I was negotiating only African American cases and not theirs. For example: if the position that Management planned to eliminate, had two employee performing the same duties, one an African American employee with the highest seniority, and the other a Caucasian with lesser seniority that Management retained. Then, it would be my responsibility to inform Management that their action was in violation against our contract. My resolution would be Management should follow the contract and reverse their decision by eliminating the lesser seniority employee position. Another example: If Management placed a Caucasian Union employee in the place of a Supervisor, allowing that employee to supervise another Union employee, it would be a violation of our contract. No Union employee can supervise another Union employee. Then it would be my duty to inform Management that they are in violation of our Contact Agreement and the resolution would be to hire the Union employee as the Supervisor or place a current Supervisor in that position. Many times the Union employee felt the Union was disrupting their livelihood but we were just making sure the contract was being enforced correctly. Majority of the time Management did not hire the employee for that Supervisor position, this would upset the employee, and they wanted to file a grievance. I would reply file a grievance on what grounds? You have no grievance. You should not have accepted the duties of that position without talking to your Union Steward. Another example: if two Union employee has a dispute between them and brought it before the Union board, the board would determine who was wronged, only one grievance would be filed. The board cannot file two grievances on the same issue. It had gotten bad the entire Union body was upset with me. However, I could do nothing. The Union won case after case against Management and Management had to concede and figure out another plan for their reductions. I knew I was not going to run for Grievance Chairperson for the next quarter because I was eligible to retire and was planning to do so. What I feared was that this organization would place a monstrosity of lame conditions upon my friends and ethnic group and I wouldn't be around to help them. Therefore, I began to pray to God to open the doors so that management at this organization would do the right thing. I also mentioned it would be nice if all of my friends could retire with me at the same time. Then Management made an announcement, they offered early retirement with an additional buy out given for each and everyone who accepted this offer. I could not believe it because they said they would not do that again. It appeared that all my friends could retire with me and if they wanted to continue to work, they could get part time jobs after retirement. The city had one stipulation that they determined each employee's exit date. Many felt it was not a good deal for them and decided to stay. I encouraged all African American employees to take this offer because it was not going to get any better sticking around.

Ps 118:23 *"This is the Lord's doing; it is marvelous in our eyes."* kjv *(Blessings)*

This early buy-out included the Head Manager, and employees whom had twenty-five years of service without meeting the retirement age requirement. After reviewing the employees rooster, a large number of employee's were eligible. If every eligible employee took this offer there would be no senior employee in place. I then realized why management wanted to straggle the employees exit date and their need to rid themselves of their higher salary paid senior employee's. This Early Retirement Plan, would allow the city to revise their current job descriptions and salary rates, before rehiring new employee's. By establishing the exit date for the employees whom accepted this offer, the organization would have available senior employees to train new hires. In addition, it would eliminate the current stress on the city's financial budget. When someone from Management or Exempt employee, ask me if I was going to accept the city's offer I would say I do not know I just might stay. They would become irate telling me if I do not accept it, you know what will happen. Yes, indeed I did, I would have a reduction in pay and possible termination of my current job with no replacement within the organization available. Surely, I knew what to expect that is why I became unbeknownst to them a spokesperson for this offer. My remaining days at this organization was a breeze; I continued to keep a low profile assisting anyone regarding issue with our contract. When it came time for me to retire my Division gave a large retirement party for those whom were exiting. On that day, I did not show up. It just seemed like a celebration not worth attending. After retiring, I started packing up my belongings because I was moving in with my mother and sister at the beginning of the year. I sold my furniture because I did not need it, giving away some things and had a yard sale for other items. I did not place my home on sale until I had removed all my belonging out of the home. I wanted the new owner to see what they were buying. I did a couple of things to the house but not much. It was July and I had packed the truck with my belongings moving to a new state. I had not sold my house yet but I knew God would answer my prayers regarding my mother's house and mine.

My mother had, had her home up for sale before my sister retired and she still had not obtained a buyer. It had been over a year and the house sat vacate. Thanks to God, no one vandalized my mother's property and now I was placing my house up for sale. I turned to the Lord and prayed that I sold my house and my mother's house sold before the end of the year. I continued to travel from one state to another because of friendship ties and events. God heard my prayer, my mother had an offer for her house and it sold in August. Shortly thereafter in September my realtor contacted me to say they had a buyer. I sold my house at the end of the year around Christmas time. During that time, God spoke to me and informed me to sever my ties with my current Pastor and start giving my tithes to the Non-Denominational Church where I attended with my mother. I wrote a letter to my Pastor informing him that I had found a church to attend in my new State and would like his blessing as I conclude my obligations at his church.

The Non-Denominational Church that I attend is large and the Pastor is always asking people to volunteer their time to work in areas in the church. I kept saying I am going to volunteer for something. At this time, I did not have a clue as to what. Maybe I'll Usher; I am good at that or maybe I will work on Stage Lights; that is my field of expertise or maybe I will work in the Youth Department. Then the Pastor started talking about the Missionary field where the members volunteer their time and go to various countries in need. I decided maybe I will travel and do the work of the Lord but I did not apply for anything. Then one day during service the Pastor reached my enter core. He came down from the stage to one of the entrances to the sanctuary, where I was sitting, and said, *"You can be an Usher just hand out a program to someone entering. It's as simple as that, just fill out the section on the back of the program and put the card in our box."* I was overcome because I now understood it is that simple. After service I went home and while eating breakfast with my mother and sister I brought up the subject regarding volunteering my time at the church. My mother said, *"I'm surprised you're not involved with the church. Every church that you've attended you have been heavily involved with,"* I said I know. My sister then said *"are you concerned about what their doing with your money?"* I replied no that is between them and God. Then suddenly I realized I did not want to do anything in this **Caucasian Church**. Then God said to me *"you don't want to do anything in my church?"* I had to leave the table I was in tears. I had discovered I was a *bigot and a racist*. I always felt there were negative feelings that an individual may have toward different cultures but I did not know the extent of mine. When talking to someone about another individual I would say I hate him or her and then the person that I was talking to would say that is too strong of a word. You should say you strongly dislike that person, to me it all meant the same. Now I realize it is not the same because your hatred can become overpowering turning into a demonic spirit. I started telling God I was so sorry and I could not stop crying. I cried and cried and cried. Then God brought to my attention:

Rom 10: 9-13 "That if thou shalt confess with thy mouth the Lord Jesus, and shalt believe in thine heart that God hath raised him from the dead, thou shalt be saved. For with the heart man believeth unto righteous-ness; and with the mouth confession is made unto salvation. For the scripture saith, Who soever believeth on him shall not be ashamed. For there is no difference between the Jew and the Greek: for the same Lord over all is rich unto all that call upon him. For whosoever shall call upon the name of the Lord shall be saved." kjv (revelation)

God had taken me on a journey to discover love in particular his love. This is the love we should possess or strive to possess. God had told me as a child I was his then kept me allowing me to make the choice **HIS WAY.** I did not always see it his way because there were a ton of ideal's I had about God and how he related to me. I felt God knew me, he knows my heart, and I do not have to prove anything or pretend to be something I am not. I had analyzed God as I would if his nature was a man and felt like he should logically understand my wants, needs, and desires. I wanted God to be equal with me and not as one whom is **Sovereign.**

Ps 94:11 The Lord knoweth the thoughts of man, that they are vanity." kjv (discovery)

I thought this was all about me all about what I wanted. Then I saw myself in a world of darkness. There were evil spirits surrounding me but I longed for joy, peace, and happiness which at times felt so far away. What I should have concentrated on was God's love for he had not forgotten or forsaken me. I had withdrawn me from God by rationalizing my behavior and the condition that I had brought upon myself by myself. It reminds me of the prodigal son when he finally came to himself, he said:

Lk 15: 17-20 "And when he came to himself, he said, How many hired servants of my father's have bread enough and to spare, and I perish with hunger! I will arise and go to my father, and will say unto him, Father, I have sinned against heaven, and before thee, and am no more worthy to be called thy son: make me as one of thy hired servants. And he arose, and came to his father. But when he was yet a great way off, his father saw him, and had compassion and ran and fell on his neck, and kissed him." kjv (recovery)

No one has to reach the point of feeling there is no return to your heavenly Father. For he see us from afar and will offer and show compassion especially if a sincere repentance is made. Once out of the realm of God you began to spiral into a world of wickedness losing your greatest assets, which are God's joy, loving companionship, grace, mercy and happiness. The defining method to recapture those feelings is through the word of God where you will discover one can be restored. For God had a glorious plan that through his Son we would be brought back into his blessings. **Redemption - Salvation.**

Rom 12:2 *"And be not conformed to this world: but be ye transformed by the renewing of your mind, that ye may prove what is that good, and acceptable, and perfect will of God." kjv (discovery)*

On this journey, I uncovered my selfishness, my limitation of God's faith and my lack of knowing his word. Through this awakening, it was revealed this was not about me. It was never about me. Although, all the wonderful things God had done for me, is doing for me and will continues do for me, surrounding my life, it was never about me. No! It was not about me, it is about something bigger then I could ever be. Example the movie ***"Exodus - Gods and Kings."*** This movie was an adaptation of the story of Moses from one man's ideology. Moses, God's messenger, did not know that the people in Egypt being oppressed were his brethren. Once his birthright was brought to his attention Moses denied it. Finally, allegations surrounding the death of Pharaoh's guard, killed by Moses, and his birthright eventually lead to his exile from Egypt. Then one day God revealed himself as a child and told Moses he was going to be the vehicle in which his brethrens would be freed from bondage. Moses continued to struggle with his identity and a belief of a God that he knew nothing about. His attempt to do God's will his way, through battle, turned out disastrous. Finally, God takes control-leaving Moses to watch the events, the plagues that fell upon Egypt. I could not believe what I was watching. This director did not have a clue of the man called Moses or the bible, and his choice to use a child to represent God was preposterous. Maybe, the director was trying to elude that people do struggle when it comes to accepting God in their lives. That only through a visual representation, of God, can one truly accept and identify with him clearly. This movie surly did not depict the bible's version of Moses and left me challenging the director's inability to comprehend the word of God.

Isa 55:8 *"For my thoughts are not your thoughts, neither are your ways my ways, saith the Lord." kjv (discovery)*

Moses presence, in Exodus the second book of the bible, fulfilled the prophecy as it relates to the Hebrew people. It delivered a message that Pharaoh God's did not compare to the true and living God of the Hebrew people. Finally, making Pharaoh, the oppressor, the one being oppressed, then making Pharaoh release his people carrying with them silver and gold given to them by the Egyptian people. It was never about the man Moses; it was about the word of God being revealed through Moses whom allowed God to use him as his ambassador. Likewise, it was never about me. My life is to be an Epistle of Jesus Christ our Lord and Savior. Introducing Jesus through my life to many about God's grace and mercy, and making known to others around me God's marvelous, and wonderful works.

I Pe 2:19-25 For this is trustworthy, if a man for conscience toward God endure grief, suffering wrongfully. For what glory is it, if, when ye be buffeted for your faults, ye shall take it patiently? But if, when ye do well, and suffer for it, ye take it patiently, this is acceptable with God. For even hereunto were ye called: because Christ also suffered for us, leaving us an example, that ye should follow his steps: Who did no sin, neither was guile found in his mouth: Who, when he was reviled, reviled not again; when he suffered, he threatened not; but committed himself to him that judgeth righteously; Who his own self bare our sins in his own body on the tree, that we, being dead to sins, should live unto righteousness: by whose stripes ye were healed. For ye were as sheep going astray; but are now returned unto the Shepherd and Bishop of your souls." kjv (It's about Jesus Christ)

About the Author

Born in the USA, in the state of Michigan, to middle-class parents with a family of nine siblings. Ambitious parents wanted their children to accomplish more than what was available for them, and education was a must. The author attended two universities then eventually dropped out due to lack of funds and commitment. Tossing and turning in life, struggling, searching, trying to determine what is the purpose of my life. That question was answered when the discovery of what was already within, the author, personified and now defines the characteristics the author portrays today.

Printed in the United States
By Bookmasters